HOW I BECAME
AN HISTORIAN

Also by Penelope Scambly Schott

Poetry Chapbooks
My Grandparents Were Married for Sixty-five Years (1977)
Wave Amplitude in the Mona Passage (1998)
These Are My Same Hands (2004)
Almost Learning to Live in This World (2004)
Under Taos Mountain: The Terrible Quarrel of Magpie and Tía (2009)
Aretha's Hat (with Kathryn Stripling Byer, 2009)
Lovesong for Dufur (2013)

Poetry Collections
The Perfect Mother (1994)
Baiting the Void (2005)
May the Generations Die in the Right Order (2007)
Six Lips (2009)
Crow Mercies (2010)

Narrative Poetry
Penelope: The Story of the Half-Scalped Woman (1999)
The Pest Maiden: A Story of Lobotomy (2004)
A is for Anne: Mistress Hutchinson Disturbs the Commonwealth (2007)
Lillie Was a Goddess, Lillie Was a Whore (2013)

Novel
A Little Ignorance (1986)

Canine Memoir
Rumi & Lily: An Internet Love Story (with Jean Anaporte, 2012)

HOW I BECAME AN HISTORIAN

Poems by Penelope Scambly Schott

Cherry Grove Collections

For Maggie —
Be your own historian —
you know things
nobody else does!

Penelope

© 2014 by Penelope Scambly Schott

Published by Cherry Grove Collections
P.O. Box 541106
Cincinnati, OH 45254-1106

ISBN: 9781625490957
LCCN: 2014944116

Poetry Editor: Kevin Walzer
Business Editor: Lori Jareo

Cover image: Ann Pearce

Visit us on the web at www.cherry-grove.com

Acknowledgments

Thanks to the following print and online publications in which these poems have appeared, some in earlier versions:

Arroyo, "Faith"

Cave Wall, "The river is named a name nobody knows"

Calyx, "Three True Stories," "You, who will be alive and reading after I'm gone"

Cloudbank, "My Wide Life"

Front Range, "The Layered Rock," "Where a Spring Rises to Become Buck Creek"

Gold Man Review, "God Becomes a Hairdresser," "Toilet Paper," "Wanting What Someone Else Has"

Gulf Stream, "Another Fact about Ageing"

Hartskill, "The Painted Bed"

I-70: "Three a.m."

The Liberal Media Made Me Do It, "His Eye"

Marco Polo, "When You Find Yourself Standing at the Railing of a Bridge"

Miramar, "You, who will be alive and reading after I'm gone"

The New Guard, "His Eye"

New Mirage, "Warmth"

New Verse News, "Drought," "February"

Nimrod, "The Cliffs beyond Akaroa"

North Coast Squid, "How the Wet Rocks Talk," published as "Look at these remnants of the ancient shoreline"

Off the Coast, "Birthday Present," "You, who will be alive and reading after I'm gone"

Oscillation, "The river is named a name nobody knows"

Oregon Poetry Association, "Cazouls-les-Béziers"

The Passaic Review, "My Grandma Rose's Heavy Aluminum Saucepan with its Wooden Handle and Knob"

Persimmon Tree, "I went barefoot into the uncut grass"

Prime Number, "Menu"

Redheaded Stepchild, "Gleaner"

Rhino, "Shadow Play for my Mother in Six Scenes" (1st prize, 2012)

Roar Magazine, "Mother Arrives at Twilight"

Superstition Review, "Door at the End of the Hall"

Tupelo Spring Project, 2011, (2nd prize) "I Have Often Imagined Myself as a Bag Lady"

Untitled Country Review, "Fertility Goddess, Malta, circa 3000 BC"

U.S.1 Worksheets, "Pestering the Slug," "Solstice Celebration," "A young sparrow"

Voice Catcher, "Memorial Day on South Greeley Avenue"

Whitman 150, "Before They Reheat the Rod"

Table of Contents

I
Pestering the Slug..13
Faith..14
Perspective..16
Memorial Day on South Greeley Avenue...............18
The Unkindness of the Young..............................19
Three True Stories..21
On the Day after Thanksgiving............................22
Wanting What Somebody Else Has......................23
The Cliffs beyond Akaroa....................................24
The Woman who Lives at Newark
    Airport (ERW)..25
In the Day of Prosperity Be Joyful........................26
My Wide Life..27
Instructions for the Proper Use of Ferric Oxide.....28
Warmth...30
Where a Spring Rises to Become Buck Creek.......31
The Enormous Thing..32
His Eye..33
God Becomes a Hairdresser................................34

II
Shadow Play for my Mother in Six Scenes...........37
Election Night 2008..39
Old Man 40
Old Dog...41
Glory is Reached by Many Routes.......................42
March..43
Drought...44
Birthday Present...45
The river is named a name nobody knows 47
Personal Protest against this Death Thing...........48
Menu...50
For We Are as Water Spilt on the Ground 51
The Gates of Prague...53

And they brought forth out of Egypt a chariot.................54
Kids Get How It Works..56

III

Diorama of a September Evening.........................59
Cazouls-les-Béziers, 1958..60
Will You Tell Your Children Before You Die? 61
Remembering the Alcoholic Husband.....................62
Apology to my Daughter 63
Cunt..64
In which I Beg an Old Friend to Stop Lecturing
    Me about Privilege..65
I went barefoot into the uncut grass............................67
Gleaner...68
From Cascade Head above the Oregon Coast........69
Three a.m...70
Anticipation...71
The Layered Rock...72
Why We Sleep with Our Dog..................................75
My Grandma Rose's Heavy Aluminum Saucepan
    with its Wooden Handle and Knob......................76

IV

Reportage...81
Every Woman I Know Has Imagined Herself
    as a Bag Lady...83
February...84
The Painted Bed..85
Mother Arrives at Twilight.......................................86
When You Find Yourself Standing at the
    Railing of a Bridge..87
How the Wet Rocks Talk..88
Not Barking...89
Keeper..90
Fertility Goddess, Malta, circa 3000 BC.................91
Door at the End of the Hall.....................................92
Another Fact about Ageing.......................................93
Toilet Paper..94

Trees of my Childhood..96
A young sparrow 97
Before They Reheat the Rod.......................................98
You, who will be alive and reading after
    I'm gone..99
Summer Solstice 100

For Eric

I

Pestering the Slug

It glistened by the step,
chocolate brown with knobs on its horns.

I pulled out a stalk of grass and tickled
the slug's patterned back.

Next I poked at the light and shiny belly.
The slug curled itself up.

With my huge hand, I hoisted
the slug onto a wad of dry grasses

and let it plunk down again.
I closed my eyes.

I opened my eyes.
The uninjured slug had uncurled itself

and lifted its flexible horns,
and now it was oozing away

from the step, moving fast
for a slug,

whereupon, for the first time in my long
and mostly harmless life,

I briefly understood
the unblameable charm of evil.

Faith

No one lives in the empty house
except God and me.

We share it with little brown bats
who keep the same hours as God.

Bats slide through the broken louvers
at the north end of the attic, scraps

of prayer

tucked under each warm wing.
These prayers are frayed. Nobody

ever bothers to attend to them.
This one, for example,

for the thirty-day-old baby Ismail Gul
in a Kabul refugee camp:

He was never warm in his entire life,
said the grieving father,

not once.

I sort the prayers by merit or whim
right here under the vent

on top of these scuffed leather valises
where God – where all the gods

we've ever invented – can be trusted
to ignore them.

Perspective

Drive with care and use Sinclair. 26¢ a gallon.
Under the green Sinclair dinosaur,

the man stuck a stick into oil and wiped the stick
with a blue rag.

In Granddaddy's new Buick, me and my little sister
rode all afternoon,

the road getting longer and skinnier behind us.
My great-grandmother

had disappeared, and nobody bothered to tell me.
How could I learn about history

as everything got farther away?
Granddaddy's pipe smoke bent over and trailed out

the wing window of the car.
The shop where we stopped for rum raisin cones

sold enormous wrapped caramel popcorn balls
tied with a red bow,

but I couldn't have one and soon I'd be too old
to want one.

Or what if the new car crashed and all of us died
right that minute –

Granddaddy's pink head shiny under his fedora
and my poor baby sister

stuck forever at too young to read?

Memorial Day on South Greeley Avenue

Holding it high and true
for our sixth grade Girl Scout troop

Our American flag
my American flag

Holding the heavy pole steady
in a pouch strapped by my crotch

It was the first time anything important
hung between my legs

My tears scalded and dripped
for Yorktown and Gettysburg and Normandy

for every young man
who was my dead Uncle Bubs

Nothing
I could do as a girl on South Greeley Avenue

could ever count as much
as that day when I led the parade

The Unkindness of the Young

1

We were all shooting baskets after school.
Good shot, she called, that girl I barely knew,

that girl who had it all: friends, perkiness,
natural grace. *Good shot*, she said.

And I, unaccustomed to praise, stopped
mid-court and slapped her and dashed

from the gym. Later that same year
my mother ran over the girl's dog.

I didn't apologized. I no longer remember
the girl's name. Maybe *Janet*?

2

*I will help other people at all time
and obey the Girl Scout laws.*

Week one: We were meant to learn life-saving
but I hung out talking under the dock.

Week two: I changed tents to avoid a sad girl
because she wore men's shoes

and she picked her zits,
and someone might think I had been her friend.

3

Now at seventy, I call my close friends *Sweetie*
whenever we say goodbye.

Yes, of course, I do still know their real names
but endearments come spilling out from my mouth

because each known friend is precious,
like the time I hugged my old father so hard,

so desperately, as if he were my last lover
boarding a dark train.

Three True Stories

On an old rice plantation in the last hour of slavery
a Negro in a red head rag serves a blue-coated officer
French brandy she pours from a crystal decanter.

In her dining room in the 'fifties my grandmother's toe
presses a bell under the carpet to summon the maid
we all pretend is invisible in her white lace apron.

In the owners' box at Yankee Stadium in the 1980's
a Black maid in a black uniform and a white apron
offers the guests greasy hot dogs from a silver tray.

I was there too.
I sat in the leather chair shaped like a catcher's mitt
and licked my fingers.

On the Day after Thanksgiving

Last cottonwood leaves float on the creek

The lace tablecloth is laundered and folded

The arched turkey carcass boils in the soup pot

How lovely the sliced carrots, cadmium orange

Even the dog is full

The pumpkin out on the porch is starting to rot

I dial and dial everyone I love

Wanting What Somebody Else Has

With whole body devotion, my dog
gnaws her neglected rawhide bone

after a visiting dog has chewed it
to mush. The spit of another dog

has rendered it precious. Listen
to the skritch of her molars –

such gratified concentration,
her tail out flat behind her.

And what is it I covet? The girl
who checked out my groceries

couldn't see that she was lovely.
Because I can't steal her beauty,

I just stole two ripe strawberries
from the neighbors' rock wall –

so sweet. Who still remembers
the nipples of my young breasts?

Little yellow strawberry seeds
prickle the tongue.

The Cliffs beyond Akaroa

The seal sleeps underwater.
She rises in sleep to breathe.

I've been sleeping a long time
under the wide sea of the sky.

Over a reef on the continental
shelf, one wave has traveled

all my life but I don't know
which one. When I go flying

through foam, I try to guess
which of the waves is the lost

messenger and which crest
hides the missing message.

Above me, up on the steep
sea cliffs, tiny sheep dream

of the sheep station dogs,
those alarming white teeth.

The Woman who Lives at Newark Airport (ERW)

It's the stall on the far left,
with a wall and a window, albeit opaque.

I know. Women like me don't usually say *albeit*.
But then, I didn't always live here.

Weekdays the cleaner passes me a sandwich
wrapped in wax paper cut with a deckle edge.

She didn't buy it here in Terminal C.
She didn't buy it anywhere in the airport.

This one is egg salad with orange yolks
that remind me of farms and sunshine.

Someone left a *New Yorker* in the next stall.
I love the cartoon about the desert island.

I watch heels or sandals from under the door
as I listen to final boarding calls.

When I rest my cheek on the blue tile,
I dream of Istanbul.

In the Day of Prosperity Be Joyful

– Ecclesiastes 7:14

My mother's papery skin
began to shred from almost
fleshless bones, a clear fluid

dampened wrapped gauze.
How, like some great dragon,
the salamander came close,

how the bright orange claws
carried it across moss,
that miniature forest.

And I saw its chest swell
inside the tough elastic skin,
and yes, I loved it because.

My Wide Life

How a squirrel will clutch a pinecone
to unlatch it with teeth and claws,

how I patted these buttermilk biscuits,
how they steam under a pink napkin,

how Mrs. Squirrel has no appointments
as her tail bounces above branches,

how sun brightens the face of water,
how from the middle of the stream

the stream seems so much wider
than it does from the shore, and how

easily I carry these shaped phrases
inside the pouch of my cheek.

Oh, fortune, the warm biscuits, and ah,
water – a lucky woman has no thirsts

deeper than the cup of her two hands.

Instructions for the Proper Use of Ferric Oxide

Hammer a shaped rock against a red rock.

Grind the red rock into powdered ochre.

Wrap the ground ochre in a scrap of hide.

Push a gnarled root into the sacred fire.

Now carry your burning root upright.

Find a hollow straw and bring it with you.

Duck as you walk through the mouth of the cave.

Slip through the narrow passage into the third room.

Spread your open hand on the cool wall of the cave.

Keep your wall hand perfectly still.

Now suck red powder up into the straw.

Blow gently around the edges of your hand.

Repeat as needed.

Wait for approximately forty thousand years.

Someone will come with a flashlight.

She will press her hand into the red outline of your hand

and it will fit.

Know how recklessly she will love you.

Warmth

1

From the high meadow of Cascade Head,
I have peered down at sea lions,

how they sun themselves in black heaps,
their slick bodies piled on sand.

2

I lay in the bed pressed up to my mother,
and her thin body warmed me.

For the first time, I was the wanted baby,
the hugged girl, beloved child.

We lay like that, touching, for almost an hour
until her dead flesh began to cool.

This happened on a sunny April afternoon
exactly one day before my birthday.

So that's what my mother had to give me:
an hour of warmth from her body.

3

Buzzing in the heart of the sharp hawthorn
out beyond drawn shades – bees

in a hive. Adjacent chambers of sweetness.
A hot humming.

Where a Spring Rises to Become Buck Creek

I know where the earth begins:
it flows out from under this wooded hill

and makes a creek.
I saw it thousands of years back:

how ground squirrels and mariposa lilies
rose between downed logs,

how the ancestors walked
in leather or woven straw sandals.

The earth may begin in your forest too.
You have to go there.

The Enormous Thing

Now that I'm old, every day of my life the ordinary
rears itself up and strikes me as odd:

>*the way creatures exist as female or male –*
>how peculiar is that?

Or sometimes the surprising thing
starts out quiet and small:

>*a bloom of duckweed thick on the night pond,*
>or *the whistle of a rocket before it explodes.*

Look how the chickadee lifts from the branch
like the nib of my pen scribbling across the sky.

And what more enormous than the chickadee's round eye?
It holds everything:

>*the white feathers of the eagle who flew by at noon,*
>*the flash of the gun,*

>*the intrinsic* Now *which will never occur again,*
>*the way fog sinks down among ferns.*

His Eye

Somewhere where terrible things happen—
not here, though terrible things do happen—
but somewhere they happen more frequently
(and I read about this, I didn't see it first hand),
a boy was beaten so fiercely that one eyeball
fell out of his head, and he carried his own eye
safe in the palm of his hand over many miles
to the nearest doctor and begged the doctor
please to sew his eye back in its raw socket
but of course the doctor couldn't sew it back
(I suppose the optic nerve was severed and
who knows what all else) so that loose eye
was thrown out or buried, who knows which,
because that detail wasn't in the story I read,
but here's what I do know: forever afterward
the boy's hand, the hand that carried the eye,
was gifted with vision. If he touched a stone,
he knew the hidden inside color of that stone,
and when he grew up and touched a woman,
he knew, more fully than anyone else could,
all the untold dread that made her beautiful.

God Becomes a Hairdresser

Things are going badly. Handbasket badly.

What sort of things? you ask.

The usual: the Red Sox season, war, those wild cells proliferating to kill.

So God borrows scissors from the Three Fates and opens a salon downtown, unisex, no less.

People come and sit in the chairs under nylon bibs like agreeable oversized babies while God runs His holy fingers through their hair.

He clips and snips and sprays them with lotions. He twiddles and crunches and poufs, and holds up a mirror behind, until His clients look and see that it is good.

At 8 p.m, God combs out a last perm, accepts a tip, and pulls down the shades.

So has His work made this world any better? Beats me.

II

Shadow Play for my Mother in Six Scenes

1. Her Elegant Shadow:

    It can caper across roads sideways
    in its black fur cape

2. The Shadow Goes Shopping:

    The shadow would despise
    the lighting at Walmart

3. Why the Shadow Scorns Women who Lunch at Noon:

    Their shadows squat fatly

    — intermission —

4. Late Afternoon's Shadow:

    Late afternoon lies long on the lawn
    stretching its thin aristocratic fingers

5. How Shadow Puppets Aspire:

    They say *The play we put on
    was written by Plato*

6. The Dead Woman's Shadow:

   It will cast itself generously
   over all our future failures

   never again to mention
   the carved tapestry chair

Election Night 2008

– for Marian 1919-2009

Was it gin straight?
Was it lack of oxygen from her bad heart valve?
Was it senility?

Was it cheap vodka?
Was it Alzheimer's?
Was she my mother?

She, who had waited all her life for a Negro president,
couldn't comprehend it.
Will he still be president next week?

She turned from the television
to the white lilies in the blue vase
and set down her glass

and grabbed her sketch pad and a green pencil
and, with passionate
concentration, began to scribble.

Then she made the last joke of her life:
I'm a drinker and a drawer. My mother,
my confused, skeletal mother,

sat straight in her chair and was pleased.

Old Man

Sunset on his skin, that neighbor star.
The taste of his rotten tooth.

Tonight the old man can't remember
enough to fill up so many years:

his young wife,
the velvet insides of her thighs,

and, on this last night, the surreptitious
jacking-off that doesn't work,

the ache in his wrist,
the hand that stops and dreams

how woodpiles used to split and stack themselves –
everything gone to ash.

Yes, there once was a war,
not like the wars now.

The town cop looks like a child.
Mama would choke at the price of a cabbage.

He sure hopes he's wrong
about no God and no Heaven.

How he floats into sleep.
How he bobs and drifts on that last lake.

How he doesn't know he's approaching
the dam.

Old Dog

Long ago when I was a girl
on a summer afternoon

in the middle of a worn century,
I lay alone in a warm meadow

and saw I was brief as grass.
Back in that meadow

nobody came but a garter snake.
The snake went, its stripe dividing

the high weeds. That day I was sure
that nobody would ever come.

Now my dog looks into my face.
Her muzzle has gone white.

Her back legs collapse.
I hear her plead, *Do something*.

I do. I dial. Soon
the vet comes to the house

with a long needle. How I couldn't
do as much for my dying mother.

Back in that meadow. Shocked
because I would die. Shocked

by being only myself.

Glory is Reached by Many Routes

Always I've thought about death, how easy,
how hard. Like separating chicken bones.

In the schoolyard of unforgivable wonder,
what if I once spent a whole morning trying
to press a brown slug through a wire sieve
and all afternoon apologizing to the slug?

Above me, sections of blue sky got stuck
in the mesh reflecting the etched patterns
on the slug's back. I didn't tell my mother.
I never told her anything.

                    But now I am telling you
how the mucilaginous grace of slug-slime
glues my fingers to the blue of this world.

March
– for Susan Heck, 1941-2013

Under slush,
rivulets push into gutters,

frozen clumps plop off trees.
Henny Penny, the sky is falling.

A thousand miles south of here,
a close friend has been biopsied

and diagnosed, her thin body
clothed in months.

My slick shoe slides
on black ice. Now she is running

clear out of wishes.

Drought
– news report from Somalia

The baskets of the rain have refused to empty.
Crops shrivel.

For weeks now
she has trekked barefoot over baked dirt.

There is no stalk drier
than an unplanned journey.

Her three children
throw thin shadows in size order.

Last night, beneath an acacia tree,
she gave birth again.

No food or water since.
She owns one piece of cloth

and she is wearing it.
She must leave that baby unwrapped

in the shade of the acacia. It will open its eyes
in time for the hyenas.

Birthday Present

The boy knows something of death:
if you put thumb and forefinger around a beetle,

if you squeeze until the crunch –
maybe God does that.

Behind the green couch in the boy's house
a half-squashed mouse clacks

its wooden trap against the molding.
Last night the mouse ate a square of yellow cheese.

If the boy lifts the wire snapped down by a spring,
the back of the mouse will still be crushed

and its front claws scrabbling.
Sometimes the boy's father gets mad.

He gets so mad.
You think I'm telling about a real little boy.

Really there was a girl whose mother was so scary,
she can't even write about it,

so she makes up this story about a boy –
how the boy hides the mouse under extra pajamas,

how he leaves the drawer a little bit open
like breath holes in a box

until the smell stops.
On the day of the boy's seventh birthday

he lifts out the trap.
Tiny leg bones spill into the drawer.

The patchy back of the mouse's neck
feels soft on the boy's cheek.

The river is named a name nobody knows

The old people think the name began
with a *sshh* sound that sounded like rain.

After that word was lost forever,
the river battered its story through gravel.

Back when I knew no words to soothe me,
one small yowl used to mean *Mother*.

Between the flood and the long drought,
the winding river has revised its thoughts.

My dead mother's name was *Marian*.
I say and say it until she can't scare me.

High in an ice cavern over that river
waits a wolf whose name is *Forgiveness*.

The wolf still wonders, *Will she come back?*
But I grow white and have turned my back.

Personal Protest against this Death Thing

If we're lucky, the grands go first,
though we hear them for the rest of our lives.

It's not like we don't know it's built in,
into each sweet nursling we chuck under the chin.

But that's sentimental – nothing like real deaths
where you want to scream

and stamp your feet
as if anger could ever reverse anything.

Consider the unfinished birds in cracked shells,
the reddened pelt smashed into the road,

or the soldiers they blow taps over
as if it were unavoidable. Don't get me started.

But even when it's been a long way
from cradle to grave, doesn't death come too soon?

My father had a sharp mind.
He put the bookmark into the book before he died.

With us animals, it's all plumbing and pumps,
and his pump stopped.

Another good man down,
another dried-up starfish.

Rat-a-tat-tat, they line them up against a wall
or wheel the line of wheelchairs into the diningroom.

Would you like a magnificent tomb?
Or what about a hamburger today?

It's this death business all around.
My family dies of being old and annoying

but my mother was only sad – her finger
up her butt to dig out hardened shit.

Hey, the death thing finally happened to her.
Like it will happen to you, to them, to me.

We can clench our jaws, our fists, our startled hearts,
and say we hate it, or maybe some embrace it.

No matter how hard I try in life, there will come a dot
at the end of my obituary. The bristle cone pine

after thousands of years, damn it. The stars.

Menu

When the disaster landed, we had large stocks
of frozen grapefruit juice and canned yams.

None of us liked yams
and no one would confess to having bought them.

When the grapefruit concentrate started to thaw,
we thought of mixing up the juice,

but then someone said we shouldn't waste water,
so we ate grapefruit slurry on cold yams.

For the end of the world, it tasted pretty good.
We all told each other that we loved each other,

but I don't know whether we actually meant it
or maybe we only wished we had.

For We Are as Water Spilt on the Ground

– 2 Samuel 14:14

1

After the rains of March,
the worms rose from soaked dirt –

pink corrugated worms digesting
their black news.

I woke up here,
inside the rinsed sky,

with the sound of one bird
singing all around me.

Oh, goodness, this world said,
oh, my gracious goodness. Just look

*at all these anonymous two-leafed
sprouts.*

2

My lover left me. Mom and Dad died.
My wisest teachers got old and forgot.

The ancient oak rotted from inside.
The stone wall fell. But the sun rose

anyhow. And new people happened.
Of course, they always start small.

Can you believe this story?
You're in it too.

3

In the thread drawer
of my grandmother's sewing chest,

I found these narrow brown shoelaces
rolled in printed paper.

They belong to a pair of shoes
I will never own,

but I walk around in those shoes
every day.

The Gates of Prague

In my son's driveway on the far side of the country
I shoot lay-ups with my grandson.

The orange basketball swishes through the white net
like the half century plus since I did lay-ups.

Does my arm still follow the curvature of the earth?
This May the local lilacs dried on the branch

before they ever bloomed – one fewer year of lilacs
in the turning story of my life.

When someone caresses my closed eyelids, I see
backwards to the fern forest

and the great rocks moving and the Mongol horde
approaching the gates of Prague,

how they damaged nothing, turned their mounts east,
and rode home across treeless steppes,

and yet I keep issuing instructions – *do it this way,
put it here, do it now* –

as if it were my job to organize the entire world before
I die. *Stop, Penelope.*

I would like to flow through my life like that basketball
right through the net with that hushed

and ecstatic precision.

And they brought forth out of Egypt a chariot

> – 2 Chronicles 1:17

1

Inside the house by the lane
somebody measures out gin.

We dab at his grizzled beard
with a linen napkin.

It is our solemn duty
to preserve his dignity.

He traipsed the Alps with Hannibal,
campaigned under Charlemagne.

The sum of his battles
was the battle of the Somme.

Nobody remembers
when he was born

or how a country girl by a stile
washed the blister on his heel.

His only boots are shearling slippers
and at night he wears diapers.

2

In the woods at the end of the lane,

a small blue butterfly

hovers over the path
and lands and stops moving.

This poem is not recommended
for children under ten.

The butterfly understands dying,
having done so

so softly and so often –
you patient blue butterfly,

you who contain transformation.

Kids Get How It Works

Listen to a kid tell a story:
this happened and this happened and then this.

No *becauses* or *therefores*
to postulate causality.

*When the bough breaks, the cradle will fall
and down will come baby...*

Yup, mostly it's random, one thing after another
just happening along,

until we invent or discover our gods
so a man with cancer can ask, *Why me?*

Or, *Why all this rain to make the cherries split?*
Or, *How come you no longer love me?*

Try the kid version: *And the giant came
and he stepped on the house.*

SQUASH, Sweetie pie.
No more house.

III

Diorama of a September Evening

The feverish sun had set.
I stood on my doorstep, grateful

for a home. Neighbors' tricycles
slept on curbs. Cement cooled.

Muscular and surly, Coyote
emerged from the trees.

I am hungry, said Coyote,
in case you ask. And the mice

are hiding. I am prowling
for house cats out too late.

A mole scrambled. Coyote swatted
and ate – even its pink rubber hands.

There is a pink baby doll inside
my house, lost in the back of a closet.

It belonged to my daughter
in that other life,

back when I was hungry enough
to be eaten by men.

Cazouls-les-Béziers, 1958

– for my French penpal Marie-Claude

At the crest of a vineyard
above the cobble-street village,
an old stone altar where we gathered vine twigs.

The walled garden,
her aged parents dressed in black,
straight-backed chairs where dirt met gravel.

The skinned rabbit
spread belly up on the wide iron grill,
the dry air pungent with rosemary and vine smoke.

Je veux les yeux
and she scooped out the rabbit's eyes.
As Claudie ate them, it was as if I ate them too:

little hot puddings
in an elastic outer membrane
squishing in our mouths with their aftertaste of salt,

her small white teeth,
as if my mouth tasted her mouth,
as if we were lovers under Mediterranean sun.

What do they do
with the velvet ears of a skinned rabbit?
That was fifty years back and no man had touched me.

Will You Tell Your Children Before You Die?

My womb was a tide pool in moonlight.

I was too young
and still retreating from waves.

The dogwinkle snail
drills barnacles with its rasp-like tongue.

Do I dare speak to you?

The sunflower starfish has twenty-four arms
to catch its prey.

Children,
I hid.

This was our life: *What do you want?*
Hope or fish sticks?

Even at the moment you were conceived,
I was hoping he would leave us.

And then, under a thin moon, finally,
he did.

Remembering the Alcoholic Husband

With a knick-knack, paddy-whack,
give the dog a bone —
this old man came rolling home.

Like hell, he rolled. He drove. All the way home
in an alcoholic black-out. Pissed his pants in the driveway.

Each week strangers die on the third rail of the subway tracks
or under the wheels of a bus. Who was stranger than he?

I wanted to ride that bus someplace far, but the kids were asleep
and he might set fire to the house.

I am banging the old fire gong. *Gong-gong.* Forty years later
the knick-knacks are still burning. My rusty fire truck

is speeding backwards through charred paddy-whacks,
crunching those piles of gnawed bones.

Apology to my Daughter

I hid you inside the crest of a wave
so nobody knew we were drowning;

I tried to feed you with tidal limpets
and the delicate names of shells.

You asked, *Where does the sea end?*
but what did I know about dry land?

I'm sorry. I'm sorry. I knew no better
than to swim against surge, to clamber

onto a barnacled rock, squeezing
a sea urchin in one punctured hand.

It was my blood. It was your blood.
I know why you want no babies.

Cunt

Shall I explain the broken places?

This is not the place, but it is like the place
where he put both hands on my throat
and threw me down onto the bed.

This is not the time, but it is like the time
when he spit out those ugly names
and then jerked back my chin
and bashed my skull

into the headboard

and the oak
cracked.

This is not the truth, but it is like the truth.
No, it is the truth.

In which I Beg an Old Friend to Stop Lecturing Me about Privilege

You think because my parents both went to college,
I've had it way easier than you.

My big upper-middle-class accomplishment:
stretching left-overs to feed my kids.

And you've been on my case for years,
you with your expensive haircut and dye job.

You look terrific. Now cut me some slack.
Five generations of social pretensions

prepared me for nothing.
I still had to hide in the bushes

from a drunken husband who tried to kill me.
You were the brave friend who sat in my house

to keep me safe,
you sewing rag dolls with my scared little girl.

I'll never be done thanking you for that afternoon –
that was a kindness, Susan, a kindness,

but tell me, what can we change now?

Should I hand over my pension?
Should I chop off my fingers with my mother's gold rings?

I'm sorry your grandmother left you no silver.
I'm sorry your dad didn't work in a suit.

I'm sorry we'll never be sisters.

I WENT BAREFOOT INTO THE UNCUT GRASS

> – a line from Ruth Stone

My feet remember the cool of June,
grass blades with foamy bug spit
like bookmarks between my toes.

I never intended to walk into fire.
You with your hands on my throat –
it's forty years since I saw you last.

Now a lock of your oily black hair
like a disheveled crow's feather
floats and revolves in my soup.

When I was a child, my mouth
tasted sweet. Even the grass
was well-intentioned, so sugary

when I sucked on clover stems.
Now I hear that you've just died.
I hadn't known you were still alive.

Today I am busy unbreathing
each deluded breath. Gin bottles
hidden in the insulation, the stove

left on all night, you stalked me
through long alleys of evenings,
and I cringed. Please stay dead.

Gleaner

A wooden ladder leans against his peach tree,
uprights touching a laden branch. When his fist

thrusts out at me, I'm quicker to cover my face.
Light sparks between my folded arms like light

flaming through a bushel basket, pure shimmer
but broken. I'm learning to live in this orchard.

I crouch to pick through the windfall peaches,
choosing the least punctured, the least bruised.

From Cascade Head above the Oregon Coast

Suppose
you stood on a grassy headland
on the north coast of Iceland
with a man who will leave you
and you ached to lie with him
among pale subarctic flowers

Suppose
this way, that way, thirty years
pass, and you hike past ferns
to the Cascade Head meadow
and you peer down at sea lions
lolling below on estuary sands

Suppose
your flesh is now as complete
as sea lions' flesh in the tides
and it was never that one man
who mattered, it was always
the high green headland,

the headland's gouged
and rocky face

Three a.m.

Even with me and my husband in the double bed,
there is plenty of space

Even with our big dog sprawled out and compressing
the fluffy comforter between us, there is still enough
good sleeping room

Even with the wind chimes and the local screech owl
and the smooth snore of the dog, such a pervasive
peace

This is when I hear my dead mother's voice on the stairs:
I hate this, she spits, as she grasps the banister,
and struggles upstairs for the last time in her long life

So now my mother is here in the bed tucked in with me
and my sleeping husband and dog

and my calendar full of double bookings and the broken
cord of the vacuum cleaner and those Blue Cross forms
I don't understand

and now look how this thick bar of moonlight has fallen
across the bed

to pin me down

Anticipation

is the far apart birthdays of early childhood

is the shut buds of the scarlet rhododendron
before each bud peels itself open into a sunrise

is awaiting the moment when socks are sorted
and spoons are with spoons, forks with forks

is my methodical husband buzzing his toothbrush
a precise two minutes before tossing his skivvies

into the wicker hamper
is the sound of wicker shutting on wicker

is him looking at me as if I were a happy surprise
in his bed

is his soft snoring
and a warm pocket of air around flesh

and the low *ta-thump* of his heart
is some unknown night

when there is no *ta-thump*

The Layered Rock

Four antelope
munching grass:

under their hooves,
the layered rock,

shadows of layers,
and the deep crack

where I came out.

            *

Look, a slow hawk
skimming the slope for mice.

I could be the hawk or the mouse.
I could be my own mother

who tried to devour me.

            *

Today I hear birdsong
below my feet.

Am I walking upside down
on the lid of the sky?

            *

I fold my cold fingers
into my palm.

The yellow streetlight

won't warm my hands

but when I say
my husband's name

he begins to begin.

 *

Before her marriage
my daughter kept phoning.

For the first time in years,
she called me *Mommy*.

 *

I will wake before dawn.
A jewel glows in my house:

my young grandson,
sleeping.

 *

When my mother was a kid
she used to chew warm tar.

She spit it into a lilac bush
next to the porch steps.

That's the most personal thing
my mother ever told me.

 *

Those four antelope,
how they go on grazing

by that cracked place
in the blue rock

where I plan
to go in.

Why We Sleep with Our Dog

When I place my lips on top of my husband's springy gray hair,
I can never taste what he's thinking.

When my hand tries to circle his thick-tendoned wrist,
distance ticks under my fingertips.

If I were some solitary beast in a forest, I'd howl for my pack
of tail-whomping, slobber-tongued dogs,

for dogs
matted with burrs.

I'd follow those pathways on earth where animals step
and I'd enter the dens where they curl.

All my life it's been so lonesome
just being human,

marrying the men who don't talk,
wandering around with a head full of words,

but when I pet the dog while my husband pets the dog
and the dog stretches and sighs,

bunching up the covers like she always does,
and when his fingers and my fingers meet in her fur,

then I am touching respite,
then we are married.

My Grandma Rose's Heavy Aluminum Saucepan with its Wooden Handle and Knob

How the handle was scorched before I inherited the pot

how the burnt handle finally cracked

how I used it with only the metal rod

how I cooked for one lover and three husbands

how my current husband has drilled a new wooden handle

how I hauled my babies on the E -Train from Queens
to Greenwich Village to visit Grandma Rose

how nobody had yet invented a stroller you could bring
on the subway

how I was raised to call Grandma Rose Grandma Schott
because my mother didn't like my father's family

how now that I'm older, my hair stands up like Rose's hair
stood up

how I've been warned for years that food cooked in aluminum
will give you Alzheimer's

how I can't forget anything:

the husbands, the lover, the babies, the E -Train, the clang
of the saucepan inside the pot drawer

the scum of rice overflowing the sides

the years of sauces burned onto the pot

the glorious sheen when I Brillo the char away

IV

Reportage

"Why Afghan Women Risk Death to Write Poetry"

— *New York Times*

So, do you care what's outside my kitchen window?
Sometimes I don't even care.

And I'm sick to death of you telling me
what's outside your kitchen window.

I know: the usual. Trees, fire engines, elegant deer.
It's like the coyotes — everywhere these days,

and who gives a flying fuck? Oops,
sorry about that.

Which means when I tell you about Zarmina
how she burnt herself to death

after her brothers beat her
and ripped up her poetry notebook,

you know that I never met Zarmina,
I only read about her in the *New York Times*

I am shouting but you don't answer —
One day you'll look for me
and I'll be gone from this world.

A school bus growls past my window.
We don't learn.

Listen: the dove on the wire is crying.
We never learn.

I hate to believe that when I write about Zarmina,
I'm just shouting *me, me.*

Every Woman I Know Has Imagined Herself as a Bag Lady

A cold Fifth Avenue night is still a cold night.
At each corner, the cross street

funnels the raw wind, a wind that whitecaps
the two rivers.

Nowhere a bear could burrow and sleep.
Or an old woman.

Plastic bags over wet wool socks gone out
at the heels.

She imagines hot cocoa steaming in a cup
with painted roses.

It's the roses she wants most, and the heat
through translucent porcelain.

And also, of course, the saucer. The saucer.
Plus someplace to set it down.

February

The early robin plumps on a fence post
well ahead of the meadow larks –
I count one vote for spring.

My lonely neighbor left her lights on all night
and rose in frost to sweep her patio
clean of sunflower husks.

In a camp just beyond the Syrian border
most of the 75,000 shivering refugees
are under the age of four.

I remember completely being three years old –
how near my hands were to my elbows
and my fingers to my mouth.

Today, on this fragrant slice of warm toast
veined with cinnamon sugar,
the spread butter melts.

We all have our mouths wide open
and some of us sing.

The Painted Bed

All the song birds are asleep
or there are no birds in this forest.

Such dark deer paths
or are those rabbit trails under briars?

The cottage in the clearing
beckons with its welcoming Dutch door.

Look how the mother
leans out holding her yellow candle.

The puffy quilt
waits folded back on the painted bed.

What if I say
there is no dear little painted bed?

Or did you guess that?
And there was never a cottage either.

Still, here on this page,
no one is more welcome than you.

Mother Arrives at Twilight

There once was a little girl
who hid in the seam of a silk-lined pocket.

Now this grown child owns a graveyard
of old fur coats.

The world sparkles like beady glass eyes
of one vicious weasel biting another

across the padded shoulders
of an impatient and elegant lady.

Down in that sightless pocket,
the little girl stroked with a well-sucked thumb

the soft tips of her own fingers.
I do that sometimes, not the sucking

but still the stroking. Twilight
patterns the sea into seaweed and rust –

shimmer of moiré silk lining the mink coat
of a dead woman.

I want to put the fur back onto the animals.
I am the girl who needs to sleep

with her dog, winding my fingers
through silky curls.

I am afraid of the sea.
I dislike twilight. Such a cold, satin hour.

When You Find Yourself Standing at the Railing of a Bridge

Let shoeless toes curl
on grating.

Loft keys and license
over that rail.

Now point your thumb
for a ride.

If a trucker brakes,
get in his cab.

Go where he is a going.
A dry place,

There, deep water
will not call to you,

only the stiff crackle
of lizards.

Lie down under stars
and sagebrush.

If you crush juniper,
it loves you back.

How the Wet Rocks Talk

What do you think an orphaned sea rock
is wanting to say?

Isolated rocks weather under shearwaters
and storm petrels.

Even the puffins are unsympathetic.
Errrr, they growl,

strutting on sexy red feet over disaffiliated
cliffs,

over all these broken monoliths, too narrow
and wet

to have names, surf-beaten rocks calling out
to rejoin

mainland. *Oh, my stone and distant mother,
listen.*

Not Barking

I like how my dog is not barking
as clumps of snow tumble from fir branches.

I like how my children have found good mates
and are growing into their new gray hairs.

I like how the wolf inside me has fallen asleep
and my gnawed-on heart is starting to heal.

I like how my neighbor waves as he wheels
his garbage pail, cutting tracks in frost.

But sometimes I want to lie down
among lizards and wind-blown footprints.

I want to extend my ten fingers
and brush the face of the desert wanderer,

the man who is sleeping on his faded shirt,
the man who is glad not to need more.

Keeper

1

When a slug slimes upward
how does it know it is not flying?

If I were a slug
I would climb a pillar of grass

and genuflect
with the perfect knobs on my horns.

2

Once for a week I kept a slug
trapped in a glass jar –

yes, I did sprinkle water drops
and fresh lettuce –

so I could paint its portrait.
My slug was lovely on canvas.

3

When finally I tipped the jar
to let the slug go,

it departed slowly. I want to believe
that my slug

might remember me with patience
if not worship.

Fertility Goddess, Malta, circa 3000 BC

Lifted hem of the breasted goddess
like a curved basket for wild barley,

and under her clay skirt, the mystery
of gender, slit of she-who-brings-forth

Nobody really explains sex — the apparatus
of lilies, devices of spiders, the complex dance

of each in its kind: the condor's stiff strut to woo
a snake-necked mate. At age two-and-a-half,

my clever grandson had to ask: *Is it only ladies*
who have those bumpy-out things?

I should have shown him this figurine, told him,
Here is your goddess — She has made you

and will rule your life, and then, this softly, set
her down, a promise on his small, hot palm.

Door at the End of the Hall

Each room where I took off my clothes
kept a wisp of my soul.

The word is *journey* as in *day* –
the days the bones traverse from place to place.

I tied back the white curtain with my fringed ribbon
and the streets came in: avenue, lane, interstate.

Then I kept walking, except for whenever I ran.
Now the dog and I are washing my hard feet.

Every song on the radio is about love,
but I'm about done.

Another Fact about Ageing

Yes, I have lost something:
the shimmering beauty
of electing to be hurtful
and prompt observation
that I have succeeded

When I remember cruelty
I remember omnipotence:
the thrill of betrayal
the astonished face
and then the aftertaste

The last worst thing I did
was to pop open
an automatic umbrella
at the fuzzy muzzle
of my new puppy

and I loved her, I loved her,
I loved her

Now she is eight years old
and terrified of umbrellas
I am seventy
and afraid of nothing

Toilet Paper

    – for Eli when he had just turned 9

My grandson knows what's funny:

the word *sponge* collapses us both
into giddy laughter

because the Roman legionnaires
used to share a sea sponge on a stick

instead of toilet paper.

We learned this fact in England
where he and I stood together

on Hadrian's Wall

sharing sixteen centuries
with sixty years between us.

So many years

and places I won't see – who knows
where my grandson might travel?

Somewhere

bats suckle on cactus blossoms
under the moon,

and I know without seeing it
exactly how light

will shine through their wings.

Trees of my Childhood

I remember you all, my tall sisters,
tossing your shadows across the grass.

Your leaves sang like wind.

Now I am old and small,
and my hair is cut close to my head.

A young sparrow

hopped across black-top on Penridge Road
and what ran through my head was this:
somebody fed it.

I didn't think *nest* or *egg*, I didn't think *worm*,
only that its sparrow parents *bothered*,
just as my young mother

who didn't want me still managed to feed me
and get me to school. I see how a life
can roll out like a bridge

between past and next as I stand mid-span
looking upriver and down until a barge
scars the reflection

and the river heals itself and goes on flowing
past tall herons who fish the banks,
stabbing water.

Before They Reheat the Rod

In the ancient city, they heated iron rods
and blinded all the daughters.

Then they told the daughters *Every man
is brave and beautiful.*

In that city, they blessed the girls' hands
and set them to spin in the dark.

Behind bronze gates, the daughters sang
the hymns almost as instructed,

but they sang in a language understood
only by birds of prey.

Listen. The wings of the blind daughters
summoned a wild sirocco wind

so that sand dunes buried the ancient city.
What endures now is the song.

Do you know it?
Whisper the words in your daughter's ear.

You, who will be alive and reading after I'm gone

Listen up.

I know there's a horde of dead poets
competing for your attention.

From your point of view,
we all lived in the same time:

the past. Sappho, Emily,
scads of scribblers you can't name –

like maybe, for example, me.
But back when we were living in it,

it wasn't the past.
We may have worn funny clothes,

but we breathed exactly like you do,
and, oh, honey, how we longed

for stuff – the usual stuff:
love and some notion of the cosmos.

Summer Solstice

Years of lonesome, years of crave.
Now, in this long twilight, a spider

climbs up my arm, and my old skin
becomes worthy – like a rail fence.

I'll celebrate by setting the spider
inside a rose. Each pink petal knows

it owns the glow in the sky. At dark
a star will light on my tongue

like a snowflake so cold it burns.
I will close my eyes

and remember being a baby
sucking the wet star of my fist.

Why did I believe the tall blond men
who claimed no one could love me?

May this late light caress them too.

Penelope Scambly Schott studied history before being waylaid by late medieval and early Renaissance English literature. She received the Oregon Book Award in Poetry for her verse biography of Puritan rebel Ann Hutchinson. Recently retired from college teaching, she now lives in Portland and Dufur, Oregon where she leads a notorious poetry workshop.